# Sopwith Fighters

## in action

**By Peter Cooksley**
**Color By Don Greer**

**Illustrated by Joe Sewell**

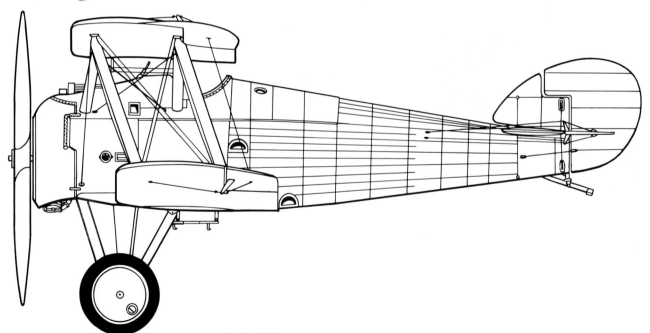

**Aircraft Number 110**
**squadron/signal publications**

On 27 October 1918, Major W.G. Barker engaged a formation of German fighters while flying this Sopwith Snipe (E8102). Wounded several times, he managed to shoot down four enemy aircraft before crash landing his damaged Snipe behind British lines. For this action, he was awarded the Victoria Cross.

ISBN 0-89747-256-X

If you have any photographs of the aircraft, armor, soldiers or ships of any nation, particularly wartime snapshots, why not share them with us and help make Squadron/Signal's books all the more interesting and complete in the future. Any photograph sent to us will be copied and the original returned. The donor will be fully credited for any photos used. Please send them to:

Squadron/Signal Publications, Inc.
1115 Crowley Drive.
Carrollton, TX 75011-5010.

## Photo Credits

Air Vice Marshal Sir G. Bromet
R. W. Cranham
Barrington J. Gray
Group Captain C. N. Lowe
Group Captain W.A.C. Morgan
Northern Aircraft Preservation Society
Royal Canadian Air Force

J. M. Bruce/G. S. Leslie Collection
Canadian War Museum
Imperial War Museum
Bruce Robertson
National Museum of Canada
Frank Yeomans

# Author's Note

It could be argued that the aircraft built at Thomas Sopwith's factory at Kingston-on-Thames contributed more to the Allied cause during the First World War than those of any other aircraft company. Of these, the Sopwith Camel is the best remembered, although there are many others equally worthy of praise. These aircraft made a great contribution to the development of the aircraft as a fighting machine at a time when the very science of flying was in its early stages — the world's first controlled flight having been made by the Wright brothers only some thirteen years before the first Sopwith Pup took to the air.

The single seat Pup was to be the predecessor of a whole range of single seat fighters which were to continue as far as the technical limits of the rotary engine permitted. The importance of Sopwith fighters may be judged by the fact that not only could they be found in such unexpected countries as the United States, Holland and Latvia, to name only three examples, but also that it was a Sopwith fighter, the Snipe, that was selected by the Royal Air Force to serve as its standard post-war fighter.

This Sopwith Triplane (N5912) was restored to flying condition for the June 1937 Air Display at RAF Hendon. The aircraft is still at Hendon, on permanent display in the Royal Air Force Museum.

# Introduction

By the time the First World War started in August of 1914, Thomas Sopwith had already distinguished himself in the aviation world by setting an amazing number of aerial records. He had crowned these accomplishments with the establishment of the Sopwith Aviation Company. His company went on to produce an aircraft which won for Great Britain much coveted Schneider Trophy (in the second of the Schneider races). Indeed, the future seemed bright for the Sopwith Company in the sporting field, with an entry submitted for the Aerial Derby and plans in motion to compete in the London-Paris-London Air Race. All of these plans quickly vanished with the outbreak of war, with military orders fully occupying the output of the two Kingston factories for the next four years.

The first Sopwith aircraft to go to war were also among the earliest military machines to be taken on strength by the Royal Naval Air Service. After the opening of hostilities, a pair of standard Sopwith Tabloids, a Tractor Biplane and the prototype Tabloid were all impressed into Admiralty service.

It was not long before the first two Tabloids were to make history when their pilots, LT Spencer Grey and LT Marix, were ordered to bomb the airship sheds at Dusseldorf and Cologne during October of 1914. To reach the first of these targets called for an outward trip of 103 miles, with the second target being nine miles more distant; long range missions for open cockpit biplanes.

It was, however, the advent of the Sopwith 1 ½ Strutter that firmly established the name of Sopwith as a producer of quality fighting aircraft. The 1 ½ Strutter was largely overshadowed by other Sopwith aircraft, but it was instrumental in the development of the Sopwith Pup — "as pretty and slick as a thoroughbred horse," as one American officer was later to record. The use of the larger 1 ½ Strutter by both France and the American Expeditionary Force, plus the seizure of any 1 ½ Strutter that force landed in Dutch territory, all testify to the qualities of the design.

The Camel was far less docile than anything the Kingston factories had built before and the very lack of stability that the design incorporated meant that, in skilled hands, the "little beast" was an astonishingly maneuverable killer. 5,490 Sopwith Camels were produced along with several experimental versions. The variety of armament it was capable of carrying, the development of the 2F.1 and the appearance of the Swallow all testify to the potential of the Camel design.

The best qualities of the Camel were reflected in its successor, the Sopwith Snipe. The Snipe entered service some three months before the war ended, just in time to prove that it was the best Allied fighter then in service. In fact, due to post war financial constraints on RAF re-equipment, the Snipe would remain in service for another eight years as the RAF's standard post-war fighter. The Snipe led directly to the Sopwith Salamander, an armored trench fighter (ground attack aircraft). The Salamander's potential was never fully realized since only three were in service in October of 1918, with another pair reserved for training and the type was quickly withdrawn after the war ended.

**Fitted with an "Eteve" machine gun mount in the rear cockpit, Sopwith 1 ½ Strutter 7777 was built under license by Ruston Proctor. The 1½ Strutter was built by a number of subcontractors.**

**The prototype Sopwith Tabloid was demonstrated in Australia by Harry Hawker during 1914. The aircraft was a side-by-side two-seater with no vertical fin, and skids attached to the undercarriage.**

This Sopwith 2F.1 Camel (N8156) belongs to the Canadian War Museum. The White dumbbell recognition markings of No 45 Squadron, Royal Flying Corps were added during the aircraft's 1957 restoration.

This TF.2 Salamander (F6602) was the second aircraft built at Ham. The aircraft was fitted with the production standard fin and rudder which was considerably larger than that fitted to the prototypes.

E6531 was a two-seat Snipe used for training during the early 1920s. The aircraft is overall Aluminum dope. The fuselage band is believed to be Red, while the stripe along the fuselage is Black.

# Development

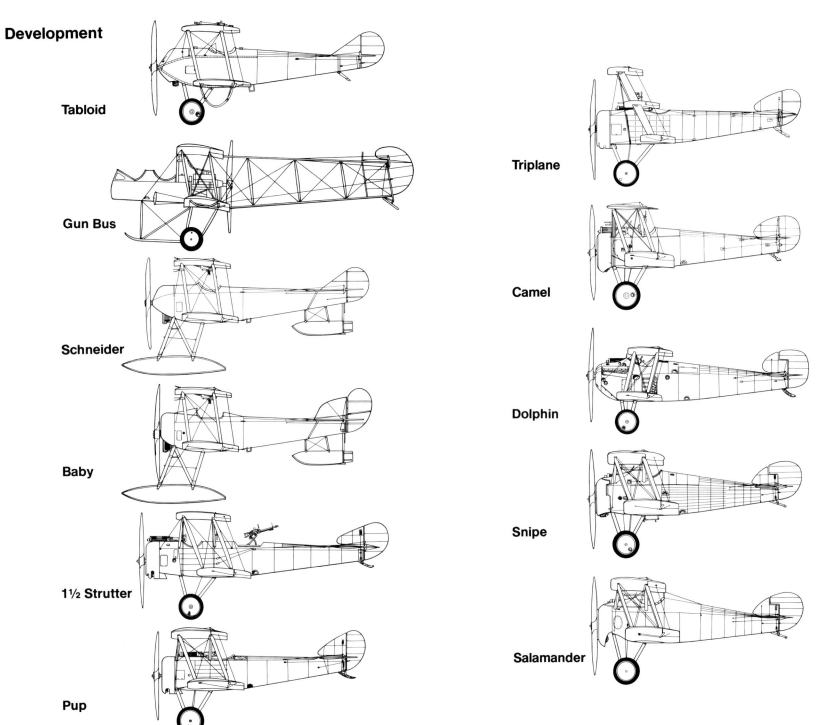

Tabloid

Gun Bus

Schneider

Baby

1½ Strutter

Pup

Triplane

Camel

Dolphin

Snipe

Salamander

# Sopwith Tabloid

In November of 1913, Sopwith introduced their first aircraft which, despite threatened legal action by some producers of medical pills, became known as the Tabloid. The aircraft's design was structurally conventional, but its performance was quite remarkable and quickly caught the attention of British military authorities. The Army envisioned using the aircraft as a high speed scout, the only military role that aircraft were used for at that time.

The Tabloid was a single seat aircraft with its lateral control achieved by means of wing-warping; that is, flexing the outer trailing edges of the wings. Originally the prototype Tabloid had no vertical fin, although one was quickly added to production variants, its shape based on that of the Schneider Trophy winning aircraft of 1914. Production aircraft also had the undercarriage skids increased in length. At first, no armament of any kind was carried.

Fifteen days after the outbreak of war, the first Royal Flying Corps Tabloids arrived in France. These aircraft were not flown across the English Channel, as had the advance guard of the Royal Flying Corps, but were shipped by sea in crates. From this shipment, four complete aircraft were assembled and it was a pair from this consignment that carried out the first RFC Tabloid sortie the following week. On this mission the aircraft were still in unarmed, although one of them may have taken a box of flechettes (steel darts to drop on enemy aircraft). It is known that during the following month, a Tabloid successfully downed an enemy aircraft using flechettes.

Army use of the Tabloid was limited; however, the Royal Naval Air Service made better use of them, taking two into service at Antwerp. CDR C. S. Samson commanded the squadron that received the Tabloids (numbers 167 and 168) and he had ambitious ideas for the aircraft. On 7 October, the two Tabloids, flown by Squadron Commander Spencer Gray (a kinsman of Winston Churchill) and Flight Lieutenant R. L. G. Maris made a bombing attack on the airship sheds at Cologne and Dusseldorf. The bomb run was at 600 feet and thirty seconds after the first bomb went off, flames from the doomed hangars reached 500 feet as hydrogen from the Zeppelin Z.IX fed the fires.

By the end of the month, the RNAS still had three Tabloids on charge. Two of these were later armed with .303 Lewis guns mounted on the upper wing center section (as were some subsequent aircraft).

Between October of 1914 and June of 1915 a total of thirty-six Tabloids were produced and delivered to the Royal Flying Corps and Royal Naval Air Service. Four were received by the RNAS during early December and may have been sent to the Dardanelles during February of 1915 aboard the carrier HMS ARK ROYAL; however, there are no surviving records indicating that these were ever used operationally.

Later Tabloids were fitted with true ailerons, usually, but not always, inter-connected by cable. Additionally, later aircraft had the skids discarded from the landing gear.

The Tabloid's military career was limited, although the type was the first single-seat military scout to be ordered in quantity, even though it was distrusted by many pilots, who were quick to falsely condemn it as a dangerous machine to fly.

**Sopwith workers construct Tabloids in the Sopwith factory at Kingston-on-Thames. The aircraft hull at the right is a Sopwith Bat Boat being built for the Royal Naval Air Service.**

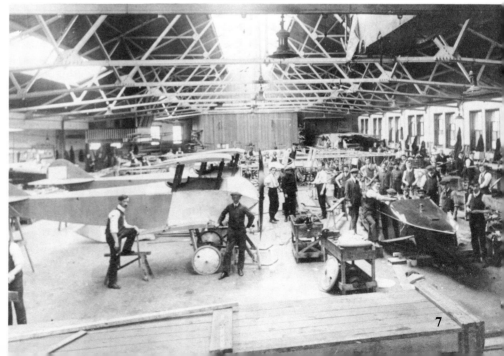

**This Sopwith Tabloid (1205) of No 2 Wing RNAS is armed with a .303 Lewis machine gun mounted above the upper wing center section. Mounting the gun in this manner kept it free of the propeller arc.**

Tabloid number 326 was flown briefly by No 4 Squadron Royal Flying Corps. This Tabloid is unarmed and is used in the reconnaissance role.

Ground crews hold down Sopwith Tabloid 1205 as it runs up its engine. The aircraft was attached to No 2 Wing of the Royal Naval Air Service and carried early Naval markings which consisted of a Red ring on a White circle carried above the upper wing and below the lower wing.

A Sopwith Tabloid staked and tied down at a Royal Naval Air Service air field. This is a late production Tabloid with strut connected ailerons on the upper and lower wing. The aircraft appears to be unarmed.

Sopwith Tabloid 1208 was assigned to RNAS Great Yarmouth during 1915. The aircraft had a V-strut undercarriage and ailerons on the upper and lower wings which were connected by light struts.

# Sopwith Gun Bus

Originally produced for the Greek government during 1913, the Sopwith Hydro Biplane Type S led directly to Sopwith's first "fighter," the Gun Bus. The Type S was an open girder float plane with the boom struts having an unusual forward rake. Powered by an Anzani 100 hp radial engine in the pusher position, driving a four blade propeller, the aircraft were ordered armed with a forward firing .303 Lewis machine gun fired by the observer. The Greeks contracted for six aircraft and four of these had been completed when the war broke out. In the event, the six were seized by the British Admiralty and taken into service by the Royal Naval Air Service. A land plane version of the Greek aircraft was produced and became known in the RNAS as the Sopwith Gun Bus.

These early aircraft were followed by a more powerful version that was built specially for the Royal Naval Air Service. These aircraft were land planes powered by an eight-cylinder water-cooled 150 hp Sunbeam engine. The aircraft differed from the earlier seaplanes in having cutouts in the center section trailing edge for the boom attachment points. The nacelle was a completely new design, accommodating the pilot in the rear seat and the gunner in the forward cockpit. The gunner was equipped with a single .303 Lewis machine gun. Additionally, the undercarriage was strengthened and of narrower track than the earlier variant.

The RNAS recognized that the potential of the design as a two-seat fighter was extremely limited due to its size and 80 mph top speed. Few records exist covering their operational use, if any. It is known, however, that a number were based at Hendon, North London, for use as trainers and one aircraft reached the RNAS squadron at Dunkirk, France.

A later bomber version had a longer nacelle with the pilot moved into the forward cockpit. This aircraft incorporated a transparent hatch in the floor to facilitate bomb aiming and was fitted with four bomb carriers under the lower wing. Little is known of the operational use of these aircraft.

One of the original Gun Buses powered by a Gnome rotary engine and fitted with a divided undercarriage and unstaggered wings. The aircraft was assigned to the Royal Naval Air Service at Hendon and was armed with a .303 Lewis machine gun in the forward cockpit.

Sopwith Gun Bus number 805 was fitted with a Sunbeam engine and based at Hendon. The aircraft serial (805) belonged in a serial batch running between 801 and 806. This serial number assignment resulted in the type sometimes being known as the Admiralty 806 Type.

Sunbeam-powered Gun Bus 3833 carries early markings consisting of a Union Jack flag on the rudder above the aircraft serial number. The flag marking was also carried under the wings. These flags were supposed to measure 7 feet by 5 feet; however, this rule was not always followed.

The square dark object above the cockpit of Gun Bus number 3833 is the radiator for the liquid-cooled Sunbeam engine. Despite the flag rudder marking, Naval roundels appear to have been carried under the wing tips.

Gun Bus 3838 sits on a snow cover field with its engine protected by a canvas cover. The aircraft was one of thirty ordered from the sub-contractor Robey & Co. Of these, only seventeen were delivered fully assembled; the remainder were delivered as spare aircraft numbered between 3850 and 2832.

A Royal Naval Air Service Gun Bus which has been converted to the bomber role. The aircraft has bomb racks under the wings and a modified nacelle. In the bomber conversions, the pilot was moved to the front cockpit and a clear panel was installed in the floor of the rear cockpit.

This Gun Bus is believed to have been assigned to the RNAS at Hendon and carries full-chord Naval roundels under the lower wings. The Gun Bus used a pusher propeller of a four blade design.

# Sopwith Schneider and Baby

The Sopwith Schneider and Baby both share a common ancestor: the Sopwith float plane that won the 1914 Schneider Trophy race for England. Performance of this aircraft impressed the Royal Naval Air Service which ordered twelve of the float planes during November of 1914 under the name Schneider.

Like the record breaking float plane, the new machine retained the 100 hp Gnome Monosoupape rotary engine, housed in an angular cowling. The aircraft also retained the wing warping method of lateral control and triangular fin (although a curved fin and ailerons were used on late production aircraft). Armament consisted of a .303 Lewis machine gun mounted to fire upward and forward through a cutout in the upper wing. Over the course of its production run, a total of 160 Schneiders were built, five of which were retained in service until the first quarter of 1918.

A number of Schneiders went to sea, carried aboard Royal Navy light cruisers. These aircraft encountered difficulty in attempting to take off from heavy seas which often broke up the wooden floats. A number of others were sent overseas and were used in the Dardanelles and the eastern Mediterranean. Others were allocated to a number of coastal air stations in England, where one pilot was to record of the type, "It is supposed to be very tricky to take off and land."

Perhaps the Schneider's place in history rests with its use for takeoff trials from the seaplane carrier CAMPANIA on 6 August 1915. For the trials, the aircraft was fitted with jettisonable wheels beneath the floats. The takeoffs were all made from a wooden platform installed on the ship's foredeck. This test was crowned with success, unlike trials from the smaller seaplane carrier BEN-MY-CHREE conducted some four months earlier. Since there was no way the aircraft could be landed back on the carrier's deck, all landings had to be made on the sea. Once again, there was difficulty in heavy seas which tended to destroy the floats before the aircraft could be hauled aboard the parent vessel.

## Sopwith Baby

The Sopwith Baby was a direct development of the Schneider, differing mainly in the power plant and armament. The Baby was powered by either a 110 hp of 130 hp Clerget rotary engine housed in a horse shoe (inverted U shaped) cowling.

Armament varied with some aircraft being fitted with an upward and forward firing Lewis gun, while others were fitted with a synchronized forward firing Lewis gun. Two different mountings were used with the forward firing armament, one had the gun mounted to fire over the cowling along the aircraft's centerline, with the breech projecting backward through the windscreen. The other mount had the gun offset to starboard. Additionally, the Baby could carry two sixty-five pound bombs for anti-submarine patrols.

The Sopwith Baby saw wide spread use with the RNAS and was produced under license by other British companies including Blackburn and Fairey.

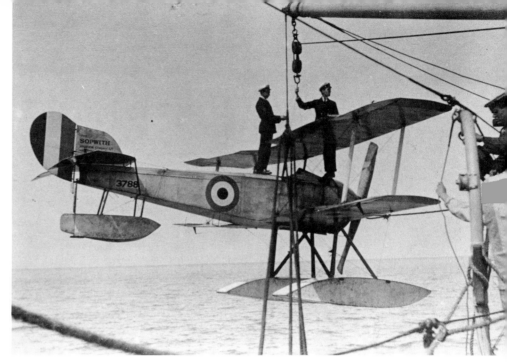

**A Sopwith Schneider float plane (number 3788) is hoisted aboard a Royal Navy seaplane carrier. The aircraft was powered by a 100 hp Gnome Monosoupape rotary engine and was attached to No 2 Wing of the RNAS stationed in the Mediterranean Sea.**

**Three Sopwith Schneiders and a Sopwith Baby of the Royal Naval Air Service War Flight are parked in front of their hangar on the Isle of Grain on 13 March 1917. The third Schneider with the dark finish is number 8118.**

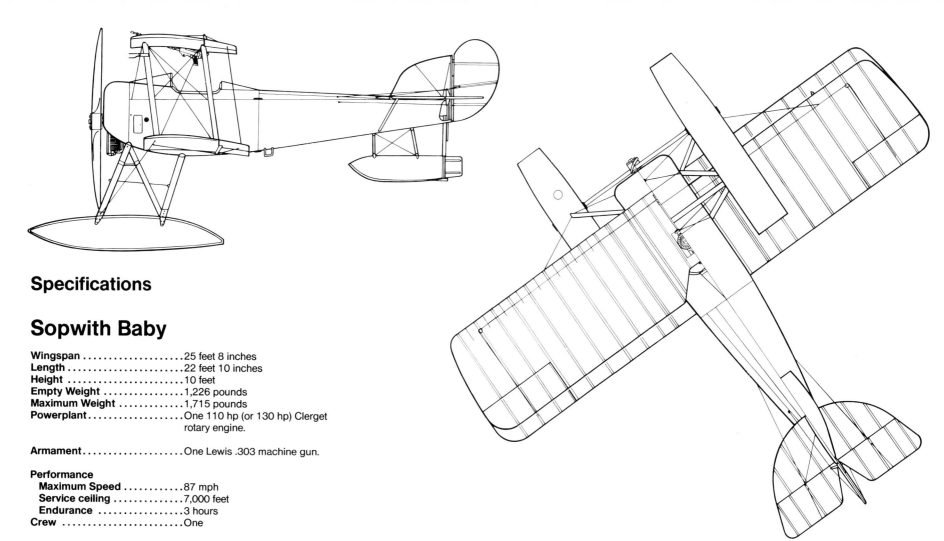

## Specifications

## Sopwith Baby

**Wingspan** . . . . . . . . . . . . . . . . . . . . 25 feet 8 inches
**Length** . . . . . . . . . . . . . . . . . . . . . 22 feet 10 inches
**Height** . . . . . . . . . . . . . . . . . . . . . 10 feet
**Empty Weight** . . . . . . . . . . . . . . . 1,226 pounds
**Maximum Weight** . . . . . . . . . . . . 1,715 pounds
**Powerplant** . . . . . . . . . . . . . . . . . . One 110 hp (or 130 hp) Clerget
rotary engine.

**Armament** . . . . . . . . . . . . . . . . . . . One Lewis .303 machine gun.

**Performance**
   **Maximum Speed** . . . . . . . . . . . 87 mph
   **Service ceiling** . . . . . . . . . . . . . 7,000 feet
   **Endurance** . . . . . . . . . . . . . . . . 3 hours
**Crew** . . . . . . . . . . . . . . . . . . . . . . . One

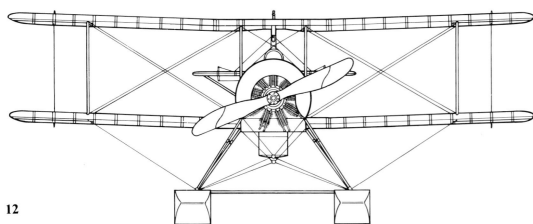

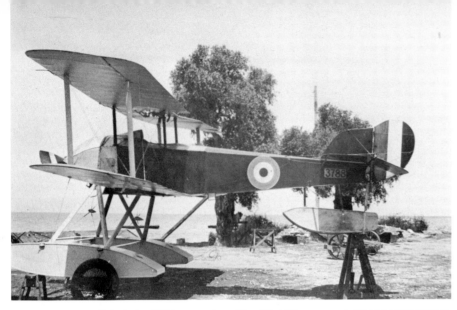

Later in its career, Schnieder 3788 was redoped in a Khaki Green camouflage and full British roundels and rudder stripes. For movement ashore, the Schneider and Baby had mounting points for a wheeled undercarriage on their main floats.

This RNAS Schneider, parked outside the Albany Boat House, Kingston-on-Thames, was experimentally fitted with Hope Linton floats.

This Schneider is a late production aircraft with ailerons on both the upper and lower wings. The aircraft was assigned to the RNAS at Grain during March of 1917.

A Sopwith Baby of an unidentified Royal Naval Air Service unit. The aircraft is armed with a .303 Lewis machine gun mounted on the upper wing center section. The Baby was a follow-on design based on the Schneider.

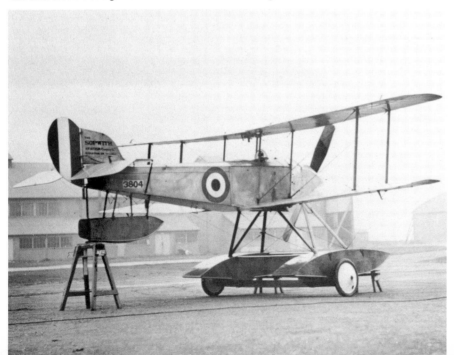

# Sopwith 1½ Strutter

Designed and built for the British Admiralty, the Sopwith 1½ Strutter (which took its name from the arrangement of the upper wing center section W-strut supports) was the first true two-seat fighter to enter service. Powered by a 110 hp or 130 hp Clerget rotary engine, the aircraft was armed with a fixed synchronized forward firing Vickers .303 machine gun and a Lewis .303 machine gun in the rear cockpit. The 1½ Strutter entered service with both the RNAS and the Royal Flying Corps, with the former flying both two-seat fighters and single-place bomber variants.

Deliveries of the "Strutter" as the type was more commonly known, began during February of 1916, with the first machines delivered having no fixed forward gun. It is believed that these aircraft were delivered without the forward gun due to a shortage of Vickers .303 machine guns because of Army demands for the weapons. Some early production aircraft had the observer's .303 Lewis gun mounted on a cranked pillar mounting; these were later replaced by the "Eteve" mounting and eventually by the standard Scarff No.2 ring mount.

A number of these early production aircraft were delivered in time to participate in the grim fighting of the Battle of the Somme and, although they gave a good account of themselves, by the following year the aircraft had been completely outclassed as a fighter by the more heavily armed and faster German single seat scouts.

A small number were used for Home Defense, with the rear cockpits faired over. These aircraft were armed with twin Lewis guns on Foster mountings above the upper wing center section. A few others were converted in the field to be flown from the observer's cockpit.

The RNAS operated 1½ Strutters from ships as reconnaissance and spotter aircraft. The United States Army Air Service flew the 1½ Strutter, assigning them to the 88th, 90th and 99th Aero Squadrons between May and July of 1918. Still others were flown by the American Expeditionary Force as trainers. The U.S. Navy also flew the 1½ Strutter from the battleships USS ARIZONA, NEVADA, OKLAHOMA, PENNSYLVANIA and TEXAS.

Besides the British and Americans, the 1½ Strutter was also flown by France, Belgium and Russia, while small numbers were interned and flown by the Dutch. Reportedly a few aircraft also were delivered to Romania and Japan, where the aircraft saw action against the Russians during 1918.

The 1½ Strutter was also built in France in a number of different variants including two seat fighter-reconnaissance aircraft, single seat bomber and two seat bomber. French construction totaled some 4,500 aircraft and continued until April of 1918.

**This Sopwith 1 ½ Strutter was flown by the French. It carried a 2 on the rudder in Black and had an "Eteve" gun mount in the rear cockpit for the observer's .303 Lewis machine gun.**

**This "Strutter" has had the rear cockpit faired over and was being flown as a single-seater. The 1 ½ Strutter was built to fill a variety of roles including, a single seat bomber, two seat fighter, two seat reconnaissance aircraft and two seat bomber.**

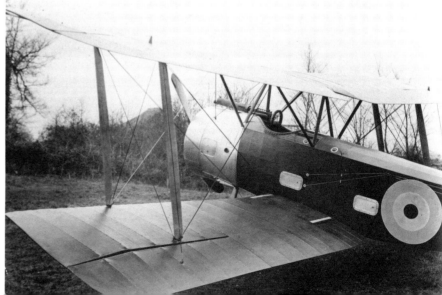

Both single and two seat 1 ½ Strutters share the hangar of No 5 Wing, Royal Naval Air Service. The aircraft in the foreground (A2) carried the serial 9395 under the tail in White.

N5220 was built by the sub-contractor, Mann, Egerton & Co. of Norwich and carried the company name and address under the tail in White. The aircraft has three lift points on the fuselage, identified by the stenciling "Lift Here" and an arrow in White.

German officers examine a "Strutter" (A993) of No 43 Squadron which was forced down intact on 28 April 1917. It is believed the serial on the fin was Black with a thin White outline.

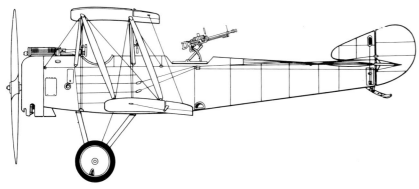

## Specifications

# Sopwith 1 ½ Strutter

**Wingspan** . . . . . . . . . . . . . . . . . . . .33 feet 6 inches
**Length** . . . . . . . . . . . . . . . . . . . . . .25 feet 3 inches
**Height** . . . . . . . . . . . . . . . . . . . . . .10 feet 3 inches
**Empty Weight** . . . . . . . . . . . . . . . .1,305 pounds
**Maximum Weight** . . . . . . . . . . . .2,150 pounds
**Powerplants** . . . . . . . . . . . . . . . . .One 110 hp or 130 hp Clerget 9B
rotary engine.

**Armament** . . . . . . . . . . . . . . . . . . .One Vickers .303 machine gun and
One Lewis .303 machine gun.

**Performance**
  **Maximum Speed** . . . . . . . . . . .100 mph
  **Service ceiling** . . . . . . . . . . . . .15,500 feet
  **Endurance** . . . . . . . . . . . . . . . . 3 ¾ hours
**Crew** . . . . . . . . . . . . . . . . . . . . . . .Two

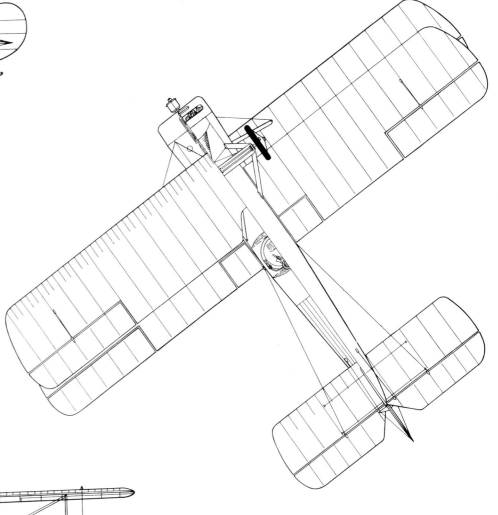

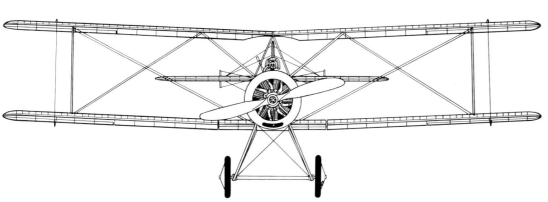

This 1 ½ Strutter (A5252) was assigned to "A" Flight of the Wireless School, at Biggin, Kent. The aircraft was built by Wells and has the lower segment of the cowling removed.

A 1 ½ Strutter fitted with hydrovanes and air bags (deflated along the fuselage) for experimental ditching trials.

This single-seat 1 ½ Strutter reveals the two transparent panels in the upper wing center section and the single Vickers .303 machine gun mounted on the aircraft centerline ahead of the cockpit.

# Sopwith Pup

Sopwith's next fighter was delivered to "A" Squadron, RNAS which took delivery of the first Sopwith Pup (number 3691) prototype (which was joined by five additional prototypes, numbers 9496/7 and 9898-9900) for a service evaluation. Both the Royal Flying Corps and Royal Naval Air Service followed this evaluation with large production orders for the aircraft. As a result, the aircraft was sub-contracted to at least four companies in order to meet the demands of the RFC and RNAS. The first production Pup was delivered during September of 1916 to the RNAS.

Early production Pups were powered by 80 hp Clerget rotary engines; however, this engine was quickly replaced by the 80 hp Le Rhones rotary which became the standard engine for the Pup. Armament consisted of a single .303 Vickers machine gun mounted on the aircraft centerline synchronized to fire through the propeller arc.

The Pup was introduced into combat by the RNAS during October of 1916 and soon built up an impressive score of victories. Such was the pace of aircraft development at that time, that, by the late Summer of 1917, it was recognized that the Pup was rapidly becoming obsolete, despite having distinguished itself during the Battle of Arras where it was flown by three RNAS squadrons.

With the Pup's ability to maintain altitude, coupled with its maneuverability (even at altitude), the aircraft was far from finished in squadron service (except over the Western Front). During the Summer of 1917, two Pup squadrons were moved from France to England for Home Defense duties, while a further two squadrons were formed in the British Isles for the same purpose. Most of the Pups used for Home Defense were modified with 100 hp Gnome Monosoupape engines in long chord cowlings which featured addition cooling air intakes on the upper lip of the cowling. The increase in power gave these aircraft an improved rate of climb and a slight increase in top speed at altitude. Additionally, a number had their synchronized forward Vickers gun augmented by a fixed .303 Lewis gun mounted above the upper wing center section; however, this armament configuration remained experimental and did not become standard.

Other armament trials centered around fitting the Pup with Le Prieur rockets. These were mounted on the interplane struts, with four rockets being carried on each wing. To aid in aiming the rockets, the transparent panels in the upper wing center section were enlarged.

The Pup was also used as a ship board fighter by the RNAS, operating not only from aircraft carriers, but also off platforms (usually no more than twenty feet long) fitted to light cruisers. One Pup, flying from the cruiser, HMS YARMOUTH, shot down Zeppelin L.23 on 21 August 1917. RNAS Pups usually had the fixed Vickers gun replaced by a tripod mounted Lewis gun fixed to fire forward and upward through a cutout in the upper wing.

A number of Sopwith Pups were fitted with skid undercarriages instead of wheels for shipboard use. These aircraft were re-designated as the Sopwith 9901a. A small number of these were used in catapult trials conducted at Hendon during May of 1917, Others were pressed into service for use in early experiments with flotation bags and with a dropable conventional undercarriage that was jettisoned before the aircraft was ditched at sea.

The Pup was also used for early trials that had the goal of landing an aircraft on a ship which was under way. During these experiments aboard HMS FURIOUS, Squadron Commander E.H. Dunning, on 2 August 1917, made the first successful landing aboard a ship that was under way. His third attempted on 7 August 1917 was to cost him his life when the Pup went over the side of FURIOUS and he drowned.

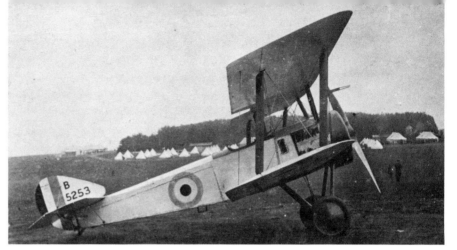

This overall clear doped Linen Whitehead-built Pup is believed to have been assigned to a training unit. The aircraft is unarmed and the vertical fin is in White.

After it was withdrawn from front line squadrons in France, the Pup continued in use for a wide spectrum of trials and experiments. Others were used as hacks for officers who were lucky enough to procure one. British ace James McCudden was to later recall how he used his personal Sopwith Pup in an attempt to intercept German Gotha bombers that were operating at 15,000 feet over Kent during in the Summer of 1917.

The Pup quickly disappeared with the coming of peace and it is believed that the last operational Pups were a pair operated by the United States Navy.

This Sopwith Pup (B2192) of the School of Special Flying at Gosport is believed to have been painted in Black and White stripes. The aircraft appears to be unarmed.

After serving with No 36 (Home Defense) Squadron, Sopwith Pup (B1807) survived the war and later became G-EVAVX on the British Civil Register. The serial number on the fin is Black outlined in White.

Sopwith Pup (B757) in the first stages of being repainted with a new high visibility checker board scheme at Edzell near Montrose during 1918.

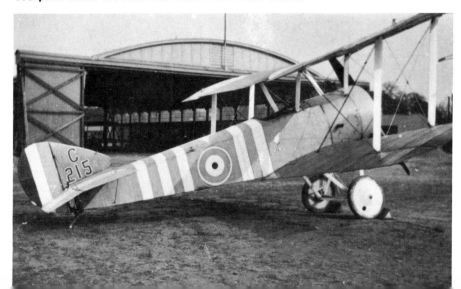

Pup (C215) was painted Blue with White stripes and carried a small Kiwi marking under the cockpit in White. The serial was Black with a White outline.

C215 also carried Black and White striped undersurfaces. The aircraft was assigned to the training role at Gosport during 1918.

19

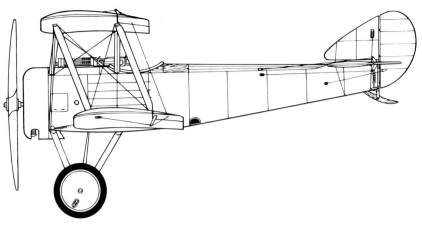

## Specifications

## Sopwith Pup

Wingspan . . . . . . . . . . . . . . . . . . . .26 feet 6 inches
Length . . . . . . . . . . . . . . . . . . . . . .19 feet 3 ¾ inches
Height . . . . . . . . . . . . . . . . . . . . . .9 feet 5 inches
Empty Weight . . . . . . . . . . . . . . . 787 pounds
Maximum Weight . . . . . . . . . . . .1,297 pounds
Powerplants. . . . . . . . . . . . . . . . . .One 80 hp Le Rhone 9C
                                                        rotary engine or one 100 hp
                                                        Gnome Monosoupape rotary engine.

Armament. . . . . . . . . . . . . . . . . . . .One Vickers .303 machine gun

Performance
  Maximum Speed . . . . . . . . . . . .111.5 mph
  Service ceiling . . . . . . . . . . . . . .17,000 feet
  Endurance . . . . . . . . . . . . . . . . . 3 hours
Crew . . . . . . . . . . . . . . . . . . . . . . .One

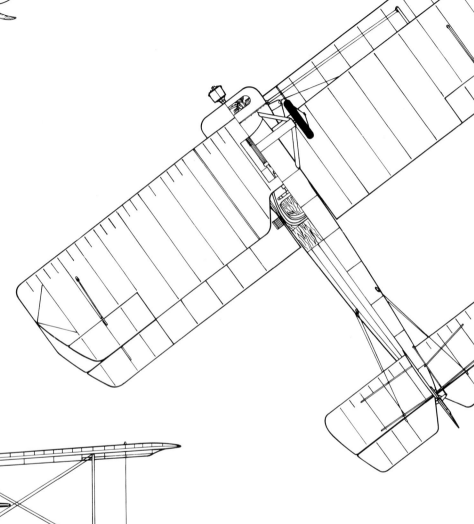

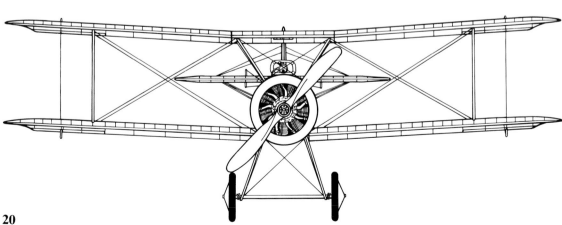

This Pup (A674) of No 66 Squadron at Filton, Bristol during early March of 1917 was built by the Standard Motor Company. The aircraft carried the company's badge painted on the inter-plane struts.

When finished, B7575 sported a Black and White checkerboard design with a Blue fin and natural metal cowling. The serial on the fin was in Black.

Sopwith Pup (D4031) served with No 3 TDS at Gullance, near Edinburgh, Scotland. The fuselage band is believed to be Blue and White.

This Whitehead-built Pup (B7525) is believed to have been powered by a 100 hp Gnome Monosoupape rotary engine and it appears to be carrying an early type of gun camera in place of the standard Vickers machine gun.

This Pup (A6228) was assigned to No 40 Training Squadron at Waddon (Croydon), Surrey during mid-1917. After they were withdrawn from the Western Front, large numbers of Pups were used by training units.

This Pup has the modified cowling indicating it is powered by a 100 hp Monosoupape engine. The aircraft was based at London Colney Airfield during 1917. The aircraft in the background is another Pup (A6235) which carries a White fuselage band.

## Le Prieur Rocket Installation

**Sopwith Pup**

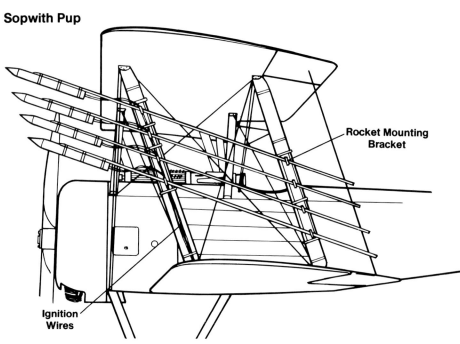

Rocket Mounting Bracket

Ignition Wires

# Sopwith Triplane

It has been said that the sight of a Sopwith Triplane "going through its paces" was guaranteed to send fear into the hearts of German fighter pilots. True or not, the Sopwith Triplane is viewed by many to be one of the most successful First World War fighters to emerge from the Kingstong factory.

Sopwith's choice of the unusual triplane configuration was an attempt to produce a highly maneuverable aircraft that would, at the same time, provide a better view from the cockpit than had the earlier Pup. This was achieved by the use of narrow chord wings, which gave a good overall view, while their combined wing area gave the aircraft plenty of lift.

Construction of the fuselage was very similar to that of the earlier Sopwith Pup, with the prototype and early production aircraft having an identical tailplane to the Pup (although this was later changed, with a smaller tailplane becoming standard).

The Triplane was powered by either a 110 hp Clerget rotary engine or a 130 hp Clerget 9B rotary engine.

Despite the fine qualities that the Sopwith Triplane embodied, its first appearance was marked by rumors of general structural weakness. One rumor said that the wings would twist and fold up in a steep dive. These rumors were all entirely false and were probably inspired by the light bracing of the main planes, although this did not trouble Harry Hawker who looped the prototype within minutes of its first takeoff!

There is no doubt that the Sopwith Triplane was a remarkable fighting machine, yet only a small number were ever produced, the total being in the region of 150 aircraft. The type was in front line service for no more than seven months, with the first production machines being received by No 1 (Naval) Squadron, which spent several weeks working with the aircraft before taking it into action in early April of 1917. The introduction of the Triplane by Nos 8, 9 and 10 Squadrons of the RNAS restored the balance of power over the Western Front, ending the domination of the Albatros D.III scouts. Even with the success of the Triplane in Royal Naval Air Service use, the Royal Flying Corps decided to standardize on the Spad 7 and relinquished their ordered Triplanes to the RNAS in exchange for that service's Spads.

By November of 1917, the career of the Sopwith Triplane was nearing its end. It was not the introduction of a superior enemy aircraft that ended the Triplane's operational use, but rather the introduction of the first Sopwith Camel fighters. The Camel carried twin, synchronized Vickers machine guns as standard armament instead of the Triplane's single Vickers gun (although some late production Triplanes were modified with twin guns) and it was the need for heavier firepower that led to the Triplane being withdrawn. No 1 Squadron, RNAS was the last unit to relinquish the Triplane, finally giving them up at Dover in exchange for Camels during December of 1917.

The best known Sopwith Triplanes were those operated by (originally all Canadian) "B" Flight of No 10 (Naval) Squadron. This unit's reputation was well deserved with a total of eighty-seven enemy aircraft being destroyed by the famous "Black Flight." The members of this unit bestowed fitting names to their Triplanes including *Black Death, Black Prince, Black Maira* and *Black Sheep.*

The Triplane was modified during February of 1917 with eight-foot tailplanes being substituted for the ten foot span tail plane (as used on the Sopwith Pup). Most Triplanes received the modification as a retrofit carried out at the squadron level. Although the changes significantly improved the control response, aircraft in front line units were some of the last to be modified.

Besides the RNAS, the French Navy also flew the Sopwith Triplanes. At least eighteen aircraft were delivered to the *Aviation Maritime* and were used to equip one squadron at Dunkerque.

The RAF has preserved this Sopwith Triplane. During 1950 the aircraft was fitted with a non-standard propeller and cowling. These have been replaced and the aircraft is now on display at the RAF museum.

This Sopwith Triplane was one of several aircraft supplied to the French government. The aircraft carries a White 3 on the fuselage side.

This Triplane, believed to be N5431, saw service at Imbros and was modified with the addition of a .303 Lewis machine gun to augment the forward firing Vickers machine gun.

Serving in the training role, this unarmed Triplane was assigned to the School of Aerial Fighting at Marske during 1918. This same aircraft (N5912) is now preserved in the RAF Museum at Hendon.

The prototype Triplane (N500) crashed on takeoff while serving with No 8 Naval Squadron in Belgium. The aircraft was flown by LT R. Soar.

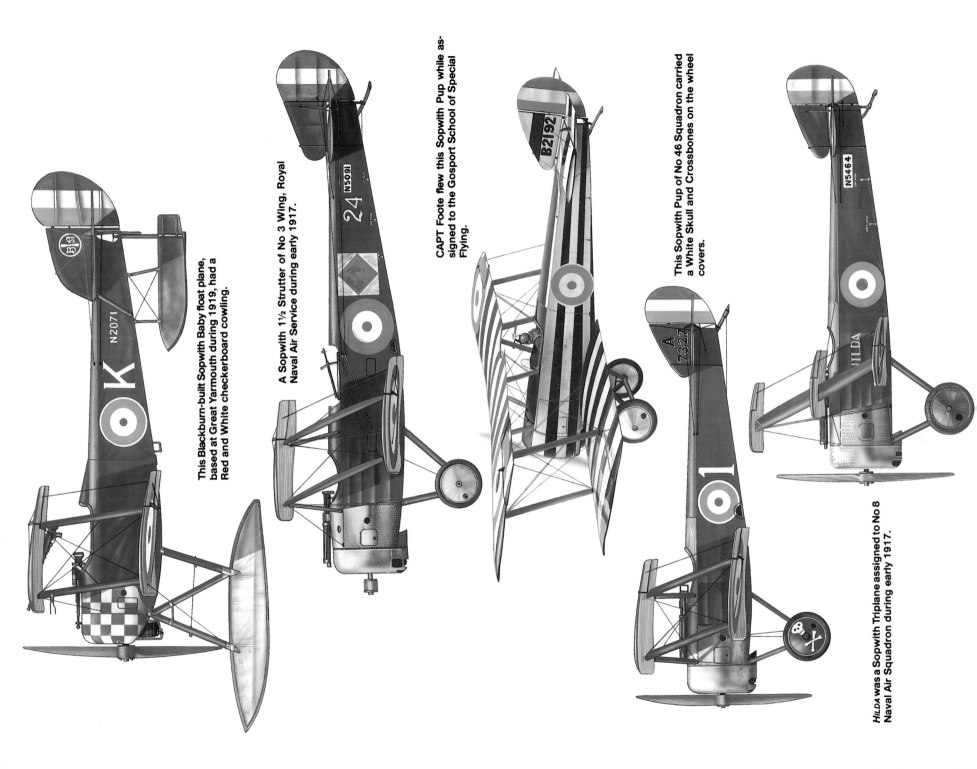

This Blackburn-built Sopwith Baby float plane, based at Great Yarmouth during 1919, had a Red and White checkerboard cowling.

A Sopwith 1½ Strutter of No 3 Wing, Royal Naval Air Service during early 1917.

CAPT Foote flew this Sopwith Pup while assigned to the Gosport School of Special Flying.

This Sopwith Pup of No 46 Squadron carried a White Skull and Crossbones on the wheel covers.

*HILDA* was a Sopwith Triplane assigned to No 8 Naval Air Squadron during early 1917.

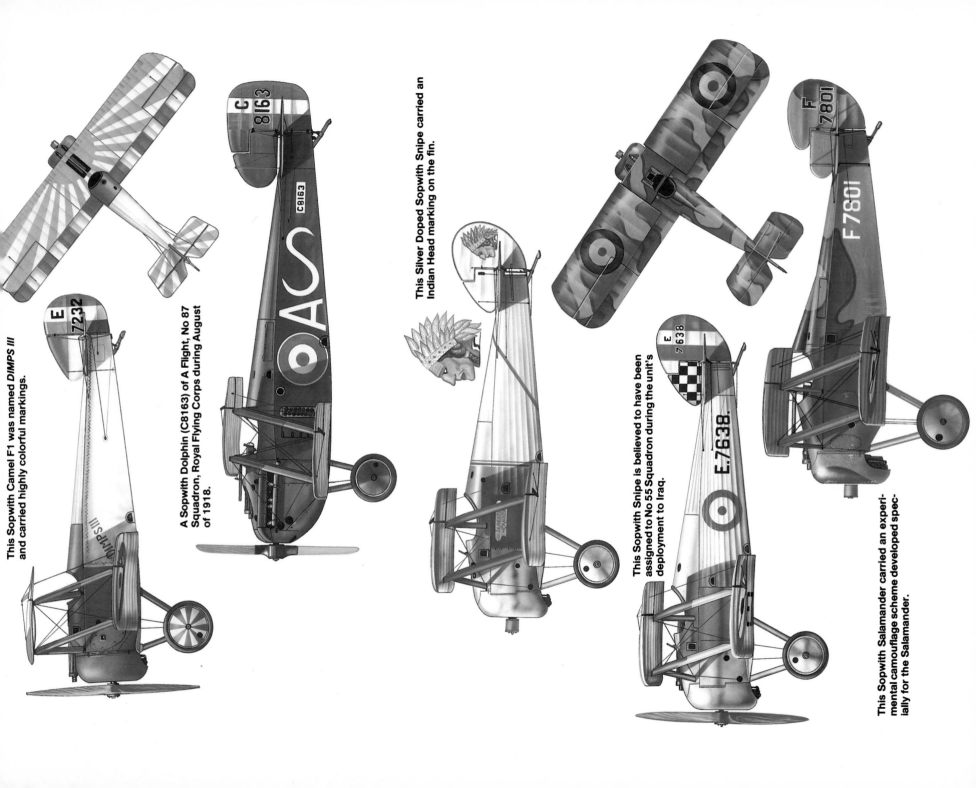

This Sopwith Camel F1 was named *DIMPS III* and carried highly colorful markings.

A Sopwith Dolphin (C8163) of A Flight, No 87 Squadron, Royal Flying Corps during August of 1918.

This Silver Doped Sopwith Snipe carried an Indian Head marking on the fin.

This Sopwith Snipe is believed to have been assigned to No 55 Squadron during the unit's deployment to Iraq.

This Sopwith Salamander carried an experimental camouflage scheme developed specially for the Salamander.

Triplane N5429 was attached to No 1 Naval Squadron and was brought down by the Germans on 13 September 1917 while being flown by Flight Sublieutenant Wilford and captured. The aircraft was repainted in German markings and test flown.

N5430 was the only Triplane delivered to the Royal Flying Corps. The aircraft was used to intercept raiders while at Orfordness and was modified with an Aldis gun sight mounted above the Vickers gun.

## Armament Variation

**Early Triplane**

**Late Triplane**

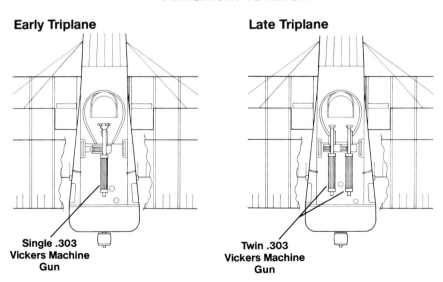

Single .303
Vickers Machine
Gun

Twin .303
Vickers Machine
Gun

On 28 October 1917 No 1 Naval Squadron lined up for inspection. Triplane (N5472) has a White vertical fin, identifying it as the Flight Commander's machine.

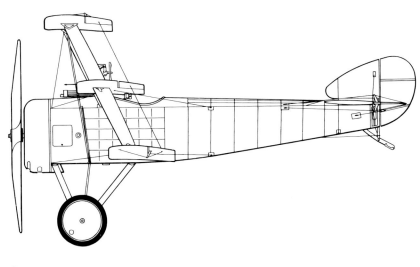

## Specifications

## Sopwith Triplane

Wingspan . . . . . . . . . . . . . . . . . . . .26 feet 6 inches
Length . . . . . . . . . . . . . . . . . . . . . .19 feet 6 inches
Height . . . . . . . . . . . . . . . . . . . . . .10 feet 6 inches
Empty Weight . . . . . . . . . . . . . . . 993 pounds
Maximum Weight . . . . . . . . . . . .1,415 pounds
Powerplant . . . . . . . . . . . . . . . . . .One 110 hp Clerget 9Z
rotary engine or one 130 hp
Clerget 9B rotary engine.

Armament . . . . . . . . . . . . . . . . . . .One Vickers .303 machine gun (some
aircraft carried two Vickers guns).

Performance
  Maximum Speed . . . . . . . . . . .116 mph
  Service ceiling . . . . . . . . . . . . .20,000 feet
  Endurance . . . . . . . . . . . . . . . . 2 ¾ hours
Crew . . . . . . . . . . . . . . . . . . . . . . .One

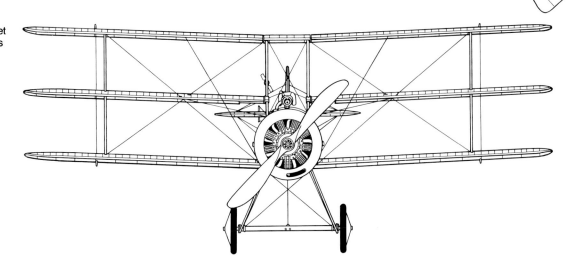

The Triplane (N5350) was built by Clayton & Shuttleworth and served with No 1 Naval Squadron during 1917.

A group of naval officers watch a Sopwith Triplane on its final approach for landing on the grass field at Chingford.

This aircraft is a flying replica of a Sopwith Triplane based at Old Warden, Bedford. The aircraft carries the full Sopwith company logo on the fin in Black.

# Sopwith Camel

The Sopwith Camel is generally regarded as one of the best fighters of the First World War. When it first appeared during the Winter of 1916-17, the Sopwith F.1 had an obvious family resemblance to the earlier Sopwith Pup. The new fighter had a deeper fuselage with a humped fairing over the rear of the twin Vickers guns and their ammunition feed chutes. This fairing sloped down from the cockpit toward the front of the aircraft. The aircraft also lacked a conventional windscreen.

The most noticeable feature of the new fighter was, however, the lack of dihedral on the upper wing. This departure from conventional wing design was introduced purely to ease production since it was believed that a single piece upper wing could be built more easily and much faster.

The prototype was powered by a 100 hp Clerget rotary engine, which was later changed to a 130 hp Clerget for production variants. Still later, a number of Camels were fitted with 110 hp Le Rhone rotary engines while others were powered by 150 hp BR1 Bentley radial engines.

Sopwith built a number of prototypes, one of which introduced a cutout in the upper wing center section. This cutout became standard on production machines, together with "I" interplane struts and a tapered upper wing. It was the third prototype that is generally believed to have set the pattern for the production Camel F.1. The name Camel, although originally frowned on, was later officially recognized because of its wide spread use. Although production machines had three-piece upper wings, no attempt was made to give the upper wing any dihedral.

The first unit of the Royal Flying Corps to be fully equipped with the new Sopwith was No 70 Squadron, which received them as replacements for their Sopwith 1 ½ Strutters in late July of 1917. A second squadron, No 45 Squadron, also began to re-equip about this same time. As the war progressed, and the advantages of the Camel became evident, production increased until there nine subcontractors engaged in Camel production. Over 5,000 Camels were produced, equipping some twenty-three squadrons of the RFC and RNAS, as well as units of the Australian Flying Corps, *l'Aviation Militaire Belge*, the Greek Air Service, United States Army Air Service and United States Navy.

Because of the number of enemy aircraft destroyed by Camel pilots (believed to be 1,294), these men were, at one time, regarded almost as an elite group. There is no doubt that the Camel was not an easy machine to handle; as one Camel pilot reported "it was a fierce little beast," and it was quite unforgiving with those who made mistakes. Some pilots viewed its reputation with a deep distrust. One well known service pilot, Elliot White Springs, expressed the feelings of many RFC and RNAS pilots when he remarked, "I don't want to fly Camels and certainly not Clerget Camels...those little popping firecrackers."

Camels were used for home defense duties where it was found that pilots temporarily lost their night vision from the flash of their guns when a burst was fired. To correct this problem, Camels intended for night interception were modified with enlarged center section cutouts, repositioned cockpits (moved to the rear) and twin .303 Lewis machine guns carried on a double Foster mounting above the top wing. These night-fighters were all powered by 110 hp Le Rhone engines.

There were a whole series of Camels that were adapted for specialist work and/or trials including two seaters which evolved for training purposes (several of these were used for ditching tests). Others were used to investigate the feasibility of taking off from a lighter (floating platform) at sea, some had enlarged vertical tail surfaces, while still others were modified with self-sealing fuel tanks. A number of Camels were also used for air drop experiments from airships.

# Camel 2F.1

During the Fall of 1917, a new Camel variant was built under the designation 2F.1. These machines were powered by the Bentley BR1 engine (although the prototype was tested with a 130 hp Clerget engine).

The Sopwith 2F.1 Camel differed from the F.1 in a number of ways. Intended for shipboard use, the 2F.1 had a two piece fuselage which was divided just behind the cockpit. The two parts easily separated for stowage aboard ship and to make the aircraft more easily moved by truck. The two part fuselage resulted in some modification to the control system with the elevator control wires being connected to the cockpit via external rocking levers just to the rear of the fuselage division.

Other differences between the two Camels included a shorter center section wing span on the 2F.1, which, although both variants had identical outer wing panels, resulted in an overall reduced upper wing span (the lower wings were reduced accordingly).

Another major difference between the two Camels was the armament. While the F.1 carried two Vickers guns, the 2F.1 carried a single fixed .303 Vickers machine gun with a .303 Lewis gun mounted above the wing center section on an Admiralty Top Plane Mounting (although some aircraft carried two Lewis guns with the Vickers gun being deleted).

One Camel 2F.1 armed with twin Lewis guns (N6812) was flown from the deck of a towed lighter by LT S. D. Culley on the morning of 10 August 1918. After a takeoff run of only five feet, LT Culley began his climb to intercept Zeppelin L.53 under the command of Kapitanleutnant Prolss. The Zeppelin was engaged in shadowing vessels of the Royal Navy's Harwich Force.

LT Culley climbed to the limit of the Camel's ceiling (over 18,000 feet) and the enemy was still some 300 feet above him. The Camel could go no higher, leaving Culley with no alternative than to open fire with both guns at 300 feet. One Lewis jammed after seven rounds, but the other continued to function, sending a murderous stream of fire into the airship. The Zeppelin ignited and broke apart before falling into the sea. Lt Culley's victory was the last German airship to be brought down during the First World War.

**A Sopwith Camel F.1 parked on the grass of a Royal Flying Corps airfield. The Camel was a highly maneuverable fighter and rates as one of the best Allied fighters of the First World War**

An RFC pilot prepares to start this Sopwith F.1 Camel which is armed with a single .303 Vickers machine gun. The aircraft is believed to have been attached to a training unit at Colton, Leicestershire, during 1918.

Culley's next concern was finding his flotilla again. He found the ships, with less than a pint of fuel remaining in his emergency fuel tank, and successfully ditched his machine near the British ships. Within a short period, his 2F.1 Camel was hauled aboard its lighter, towed by HMS REDOUBT.

A number of Navy Camels were fitted with special devices for shipboard use. These included jettisonable undercarriages made from steel tubing, clips mounted on the undercarriage spreader bar to engage carrier arresting wires, and propeller guards to protect the propeller during a noseover landing.

After the war the Camel was rapidly phased out of service and replaced by the Sopwith Snipe and only two Camels, both F.1s, were placed on the British Civil Register.

# American Sopwith Camels

During August of 1918 a number of Sopwith F.1 Camels were earmarked for service with the United States Air Service. At least sixty-six were drawn from British stocks and issued to the 17th Aero Squadron.

The United States Navy is also known to have had at least six F.1 Camels. Two were aboard USS TEXAS and one was allocated to USS ARKANSAS. One aircraft (A-5721) and possibly others had a hydrovane mounted in front of the main landing gear and Grain flotation equipment mounted beneath the fronts of the lower longerons.

**The upper wing of this Camel F.1 (B7380) was painted to represent the Egyptian god Behudet. The aircraft was the 1,000th aircraft off the Ruston Proctor production line, being delivered on 4 January 1918. The Camel carried the name Ruston Proctor on the cowl ring in Black.**

This Camel (B3926) of the Royal Naval Air Service was named *Happy Hawkins* and based at RNAS Sandown on the Isle of Wright during 1918. It was flown by D. M. B. Galbraith (DSC and Bar) an ace with fourteen victories to his credit while attached to No 8 Naval Squadron. He later served with No 204 Training Depot Station at Eastchurch.

31

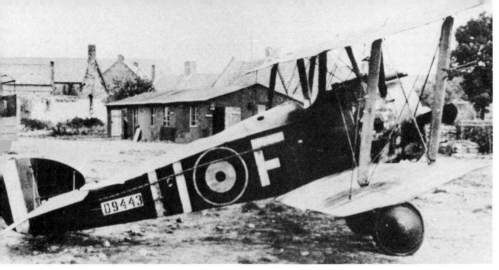

This Boulton & Paul-built Camel (D9443) is believed to have been powered by a 110 hp (long stroke) Clerget rotary engine. The aircraft carries the markings of No 3 Squadron RAF and has Red wheel covers indicating it was assigned to "A" Flight.

This F.1 Camel (F6302) survived the war and was entered on the British Civil Register on 9 August 1922 as G-EBER. The aircraft crashed some three months later on 4 November and was totally destroyed.

N6345, an early production F.1 Camel, was named *Chu Chin Chow* after a popular stage show of the period that ran for 2,238 performances while in London.

This Camel named *Tsing Tau* carried an undersize serial number (B5243) on the rear fuselage in White and the Eagle insignia of the Royal Naval Air Service.

This Sopwith 2F.1 Camel (N6812) was flown by LT S. D. Culley on 31 July 1918 when he destroyed Zeppelin L53. The Camel was launched from a lighter at sea to perform the interception.

A ground crewman pulls through the propeller of this 2F.1 Camel (N7376) of the Royal Canadian Air Force Exhibition Flight. The aircraft was preparing to conduct a demonstration flight at Camp Borden, Toronto, during 1928.

## Armament

### Camel F.1

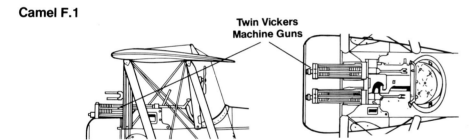

Twin Vickers Machine Guns

### Camel 2F.1

Single Lewis Mount

Upper Wing Cutout

Twin Lewis Mount

This Sopwith Camel once belonged to Hollywood film maker and aerobatic pilot, Frank Tallman. The aircraft carried the serial N6254 and was used in a large number of Hollywood aviation motion pictures including the Warner Brothers film, "Hell Bent for Glory."

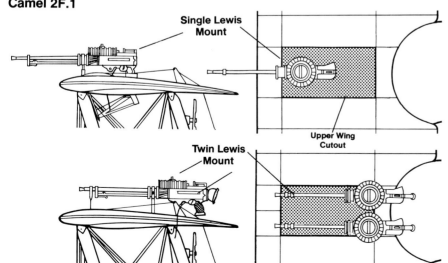

# Sopwith Dolphin

The Sopwith 5F.1 Dolphin represented a radical departure from previous Sopwith fighters in that it was powered by a liquid cooled power plant, the eight cylinder 200 hp Hispano-Suiza. These engines were to later earn the aircraft an undeserved reputation for poor reliability because of the engine reduction gears. These gears, which had been accepted as up to standard, had improperly hardened pinions which often broke under stress and caused a number of engine failures.

The prototype appeared during the late Spring of 1917. It differed from production variants in having a frontal radiator and a fin and rudder that resembled that used on the Camel. Both were changed on the production aircraft, with the radiators being relocated to each side of the fuselage.

The most pronounced feature of the Dolphin was its negative, or back staggered wings. This wing arrangement was arrived at because the position of the upper mainplane had been decided by the position of the pilot's cockpit. With the pilot's head centered where a wing center section would normally be, he had an unrivalled field of view, far better than any biplane fighter then in service. To maintain this arrangement of the top wing, aerodynamic considerations dictated that the location of the lower wing had to be forward of the top wing.

The Dolphin was armed with a pair of fixed forward firing Vickers .303 machine guns synchronized to fire through the propeller and two .303 Lewis machine guns mounted on the top wing center section framing, angled to fire upward at 45°. At the time, this armament of four machine guns made the Dolphin one of the most heavily armed fighters of the war. In service, however, the Lewis guns were usually removed to save weight. One squadron, No 87, kept the Lewis guns, relocating the guns to the lower wing outside the propeller arc.

After three additional prototypes had been constructed and successfully tested, the Dolphin was ordered into production. The first Dolphins were issued to No 19 Squadron, Royal Flying Corps. Four RFC units operated the Dolphin until the Armistice. Additionally, a further seven aircraft were assigned to No 141 for Home Defense duty.

At first the Dolphin was not popular with its pilots, a fact that could, in part, be attributed to its wing arrangement being similar to that of the DH5. Experience with this aircraft had shown that this type of wing arrangement meant that the pilot was usually trapped if the aircraft turned over on landing and the risk of head injuries was high.

The installation of break-out panels in the fuselage sides and the fitting of crash pylons (there were several different styles) went a long way toward restoring pilot confidence in the aircraft. Supporters of the Dolphin were strongly influenced by its warm and comfortable cockpit and its performance. It was remarked that the Dolphin had outstanding performance at high altitude and was more maneuverable that the S.E. 5a.

It was these characteristics that MAJ A.D. Carter of No 19 Squadron found useful. He reportedly flew his machine with such fearlessness and dash that he achieved a total of thirty-one victories in a little over three months while flying the Dolphin.

Dolphins also equipped No 1 Squadron of the Canadian Air Force. It is also known that a license was granted and production began on a French variant known as the Dolphin II. This aircraft had a direct drive Hispano engine and had excellent performance; however, it appears that none were delivered from French factories before the war ended.

A Dolphin III also existed, using the original engine with the reduction gear removed and an opposite rotation propeller installed. There was also a two seat trainer variant. The Dolphin, however, was quickly phased out after the War ended with the last aircraft serving with the Army of Occupation, based at Bickendorf.

Little is known of the five aircraft purchased by the American Expeditionary Force. These might possibly have lasted longer than their British counterparts, having only been purchased during October of 1918.

**A line-up of partially-completed Sopwith 5F.1 Dolphin IIIs in the Hooper factory. Hooper was one of the sub-contractors that built the Dolphin under license, The Dolphin III was powered by a de-geared Haspano-Suiza in-line engine.**

This pristine, yet-to-be-serial-numbered Sopwith Dolphin is believed to be the fourth prototype during its testing at Martlesham Heath. The fuselage decking is lower than that of the third prototype.

This Dolphin is believed to have been assigned to the School of Aerial Fighting at Marske. The aircraft carries a Black and White face painted on the cowling, a large number 124 in White on the fuselage side and repeated in Black under the port lower wing. It is believed that the wheel covers are also Black and White.

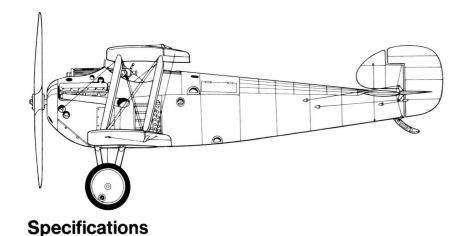

## Specifications

# Sopwith Dolphin

**Wingspan** . . . . . . . . . . . . . . . . . . . .32 feet 6 inches
**Length** . . . . . . . . . . . . . . . . . . . . . .22 feet 3 inches
**Height** . . . . . . . . . . . . . . . . . . . . . . .8 feet 6 inches
**Maximum Weight** . . . . . . . . . . . .2,003 pounds (2 Vickers guns)
**Powerplants** . . . . . . . . . . . . . . . .One 200hp (220 hp or 300 hp engine
optional) Hispano-Suiza liquid
cooled in-line engine.

**Armament** . . . . . . . . . . . . . . . . . . .Two Vickers .303 machine guns and
two Lewis .303 machine guns (Lewis
guns normally removed).

**Performance**
  **Maximum Speed** . . . . . . . . . . . .128 mph (2 Vickers guns)
  **Service ceiling** . . . . . . . . . . . . . .21,000 feet
  **Endurance** . . . . . . . . . . . . . . . . . 2 hours
**Crew** . . . . . . . . . . . . . . . . . . . . . . .One

A Hooper-built Dolphin (D5315) of No 23 Squadron on the Advanced Landing Ground at Foucaucourt during September of 1918.

This Dolphin has been modified with a prominent non-standard crash pylon installed over the open wing center section. Additionally, the crash pylon has been used to mount a .303 Lewis machine gun on a pivoting mount.

Twin .303 Lewis guns were standard on production Dolphins, although the Norman vane sights were seldom carried by operational machines. The twin Lewis guns, plus the twin Vickers guns made the Sopwith 5F.1 Dolphin a formidable fighting machine. In service, the Lewis guns were usually removed.

The White square on the fuselage of this Dolphin (C8049) identifies it as being assigned to No 79 Squadron at Bickendorf during March 1918. The aircraft carries the individual identification letter Y in White, which is repeated on the upper fuselage decking.

This Dolphin (C3785) still carries the twin Lewis gun armament above the wing center section. The aircraft carried a "mouth" marking and was one of two Dolphins transferred to the Royal Naval Air Service.

Assigned to No 79 Squadron this Dolphin (D3584) was built by Hooper, a builder of customized car bodies. The aircraft was flown by F. W. Gillette.

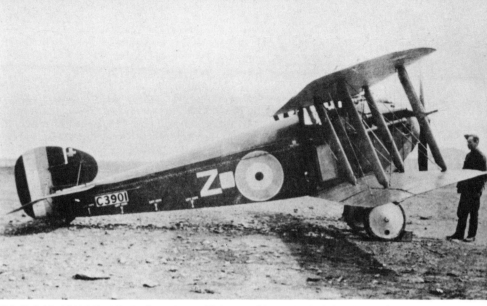

This Dolphin (C3901) of No 79 Squadron at Bickendorf, lacks the individual aircraft letter on the upper fuselage decking. The small White lettering on the rear fuselage reads "Lift Here" with an arrow in White below it.

The Dolphin's normal armament consisted of twin forward firing Vickers .303 machine guns aimed with the aid of an Aldis gunsight.

This Dolphin (C3905) was captured and stripped of its wheel covers and tires. The aircraft was formerly assigned to No 23 Squadron. The squadron marking was a White individual letter on a Black disc.

# Sopwith Snipe

With the pace of aircraft advancement during the First World War, it was only a matter of time before the Sopwith Camel would be outclassed as a fighter. With this in mind, Sopwith began work on a replacement during mid-1917 It was decided early on that the new aircraft would use the same Bentley rotary engine that was employed in the later variants of the Camel.

The first prototype of the new machine was built during the Summer of 1917 and was followed by an additional five pre-production aircraft. The first two prototypes of the new fighter bore a strong similarity to the Camel having single bay wings, a slab sided fuselage and a distinctly Camel-like fin and rudder. The third prototype featured redesigned vertical tail surfaces and a faired in fuselage. The wings were changed to a two bay interplane strut configuration with a 4 foot 3 inch increase in wing span over the first two prototypes.

Armament originally consisted of a pair of .303 Vickers machine guns with 750 rounds per gun fixed to fire forward and a Lewis machine gun with 250 rounds mounted to pivot upward. Later, the Lewis gun was deleted from production aircraft and the standard armament became a pair of forward firing Vickers guns.

For its time, the Snipe was, by single seat standards, a large and powerful aircraft. Pilots graduating to it from the smaller Camel described the change as like driving a truck after having driven a sports car. Deliveries of production aircraft began during the Summer of 1918 shortly after the formation of the Royal Air Force (April of 1918). No 43 Squadron, RAF was the first unit to be equipped with the type and made their initial operational sortie on 23 September 1918. The fin and rudder of these production variants was considerably larger than the prototypes. This was done to restore lateral control to the aircraft after it was found to suffer badly from the torque of the 230 hp Bentley engine.

The Snipe featured a number of advanced items as standard equipment including oxygen and electrical heating. For night flying, navigation lights could be fitted which proved useful for the Snipes retained for Home Defense night interceptions. These night-fighters also carried flares under the lower wing tips. Snipe pilots were to use the Guardian Angel type parachute, which necessitated a special compartment be added to the fuselage decking for the stowage of the parachute canopy; however, the war ended before this modification could be introduced on production aircraft.

Shortly after No 43 Squadron re-equipped with Snipes, they were issued to No 4 Squadron of the Australian Flying Corps. Only one other squadron re-equipped with the Snipe before the Armistice, No 28 Squadron, RAF. Four other squadrons, Nos 37, 78, 112 and 143 were not re-equipped with Snipes until after the war ended. These squadrons received late production aircraft which were modified with an enlarged fin and rudder, revised horizontal tail surfaces and inversely tapered, horn-balanced ailerons. These modifications improved the aircraft's control responses which had not been considered completely satisfactory by service pilots.

The most famous Snipe was the aircraft (E8102) flown by MAJ W. G. Barker while attached to No 201 Squadron, RAF, a Camel squadron. Ten days after being attached to the unit, on 27 October 1918, Barker was on patrol over the Western Front and engaged an enemy two-seater which he destroyed. In this engagement he sustaining a wound in the thigh from a burst fired by the pilot of a Fokker D.VII. This caused him to spin down, pulling out in the middle of a formation of some fifteen Fokker D.VIIs. He shot one down despite receiving a second wound in the left thigh. Again he fainted and when he came to, he found himself in with another group of Fokkers. He shot one down before being

wounded a third time in the left elbow which once more caused him to lose consciousness from the pain.

When he regained consciousness, Barker found himself the target of a fresh enemy formation. He managed to send one of his attackers down in flames before diving away. After breaking through another enemy formation he crash landed just inside the British lines. On 30 November, Barker was sufficiently recovered from his wounds to receive the Victoria Cross from King George V at Buckingham Palace. His Snipe was recovered and the fuselage of this aircraft is preserved in Canada.

With the end of the First World War, the Sopwith Snipe became the standard post-war RAF fighter. The Snipe served with Nos 1, 2, 17, 19, 23, 25, 29, 32, 43, 56 and 111 Squadrons, with a total of 1,600 aircraft being produced. A number of post-war Snipes were to see active services abroad, including those of Nos 25 and 56 Squadrons which deployed to Turkey during 1922 at the time of the Chanak crisis. Other Snipes were used in Iraq, mainly in the ground attack role against rebel tribesmen during 1925.

In addition to the single-seat Snipe, an unarmed two-seat variant was also produced to serve as an operational trainer and most fighter squadrons had one or two on strength. The majority of the two-seaters, however, served at the Central Flying School and with Nos 1 and 2 Flying Training Schools.

At the time of the Armistice, a revised variant of the standard single-seat Snipe was being developed. This aircraft, designated the Snipe Ia, was intended for the long-range escort role for use by the Independent Air Force. The Snipe Ia featured a large fuel tank installed beneath the pilot's seat. With the increased fuel supply the aircraft's endurance was extended to four and one half hours. The rearward shift in the center of gravity was compensated for by giving the wings a slight sweepback.

**E8102 was the Sopwith 7F.1 Snipe flown by MAJ W. G. Barker during the engagement on 27 October 1918 that won him the Victoria Cross. The aircraft was salvaged following the fight and the fuselage is still preserved in Canada.**

Had the war lasted, the Snipe was envisioned, by the RAF, as being the replacement aircraft for all the Sopwith Camel variants in use, including those used as shipboard fighters. Just before the war ended, one Snipe was fitted with jettisonable wheels and a hydrovane to be used for ditching trials. About this same time, another pair was reportedly allocated to the Royal Navy for service with the Grand Fleet.

The end of the war did not immediately put an end to the use of the Snipe in the naval role. During 1919, one Snipe was fitted with floatation gear under the front of the lower longerons and slinging equipment above the wing center section. Three years later, another Snipe was set aside for testing carrier deck landing techniques.

There was little use of the Snipe outside the RAF, although five aircraft were briefly entered on the British Civil Register and three were entered for the Aerial Derby of 1920.

Additionally, a number of Snipes were sent abroad. One of these, E8213, was intended to be donated to Canada by the city of Leicester, England, during February of 1919. But before the presentation could take place, the aircraft was loaned to H. G. Quigley for use in the Toronto to New York Air Race. In the event, it crashed on 25 August, before the race. At least one Snipe was tested by the U.S. Air Service at McCook Field. There are two known surviving Snipes in North America, one of these having survived as a result of its use in early Hollywood motion pictures.

This Snipe (F2336) of 208 Squadron is a late production aircraft which featured horn balanced upper ailerons. The aircraft has a locally produced modification, a small conical shaped propeller spinner.

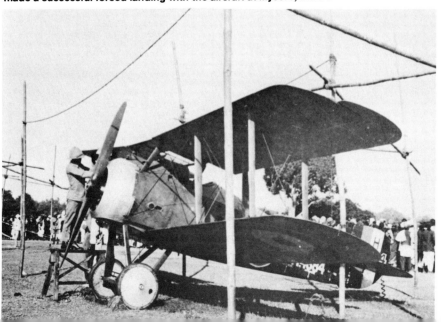

This Snipe (H4884) was assigned to No 1 Squadron and flown by Flight Officer Soden. He made a successful forced landing with the aircraft at Mysore, India on 1 November 1920.

The three White fuselage bands identify this Snipe (E8057) as being assigned to No 70 Squadron at Bickendorf. The stripes around the Gray cowling are also in White. This is an early production aircraft with the early style fin and rudder and plain upper ailerons.

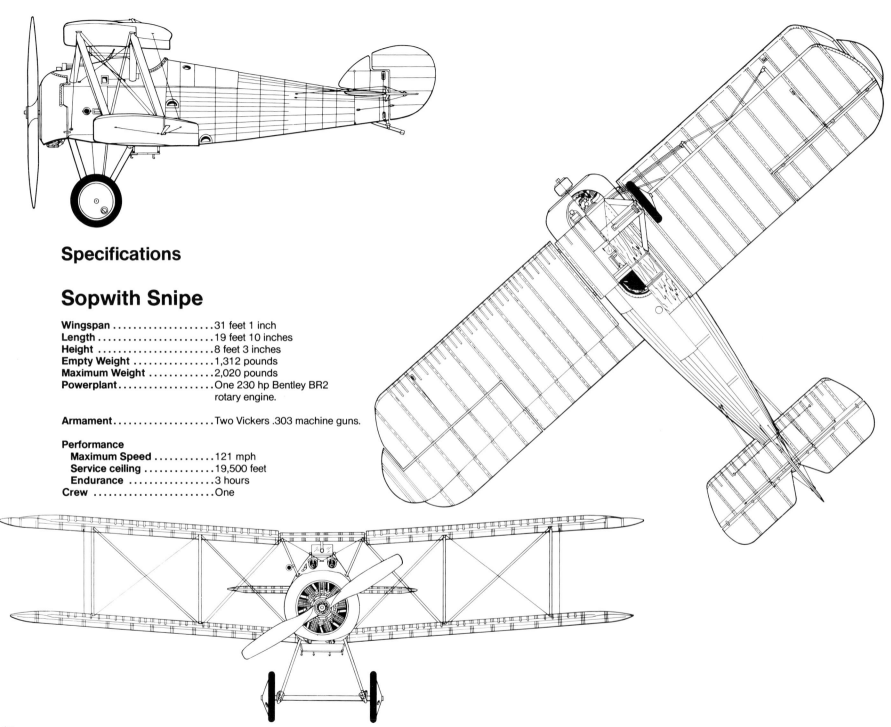

## Specifications

## Sopwith Snipe

Wingspan . . . . . . . . . . . . . . . . . . . .31 feet 1 inch
Length . . . . . . . . . . . . . . . . . . . . . .19 feet 10 inches
Height . . . . . . . . . . . . . . . . . . . . . .8 feet 3 inches
Empty Weight . . . . . . . . . . . . . . .1,312 pounds
Maximum Weight . . . . . . . . . . . .2,020 pounds
Powerplant . . . . . . . . . . . . . . . . . .One 230 hp Bentley BR2
rotary engine.

Armament . . . . . . . . . . . . . . . . . . .Two Vickers .303 machine guns.

Performance
  Maximum Speed . . . . . . . . . . . .121 mph
  Service ceiling . . . . . . . . . . . . . .19,500 feet
  Endurance . . . . . . . . . . . . . . . . .3 hours
Crew . . . . . . . . . . . . . . . . . . . . . . .One

Named *LEICESTER-CANDAS*, this Snipe (E8313) was painted in Blue and Silver, with Red trim and carried an Indian head on the rudder. The aircraft was lent to H. G. Quigley for the 1919 Toronto-New York Air Race but crashed on 25 August.

This overall Aluminum doped 7F.1 Snipe (E6837) from No 5 Flying Training School at Sealand during the early 1920s was piloted by Flying Officer the Earl of Bandon.

This Sopwith 7F.1 Snipe is believed to be the second prototype which differed from production variants in having a slab-sided fuselage. The Snipe was regarded as the ultimate wartime Sopwith fighter.

43

This Snipe 5F.1 (E6938) was preserved in Canada as a museum exhibit. Later it was restored to airworthy condition and flew until only a few years ago, after which it was returned to museum display.

This Snipe (E8076) was attached to a Home Defense unit. The aircraft was flown at night and had navigation lights installed above the lower wing tips and flare brackets installed below the wing tips.

Tied down on the grass at Aulnoy airfield, this Snipe (F2341) has a bomb on the fuselage centerline. The aircraft was used in the ground attack role.

# Sopwith Salamander

Had it not been doomed by an unreliable engine, the Sopwith Dragon, a re-engined variant of the Snipe, was to have been the standard post-war RAF fighter. In the event, the Dragon never entered service; however, Sopwith was more successful with another variant of the Snipe, a flat-sided ground attack aircraft named the TF.2 Salamander.

The TF.2 Salamander was intended to be a follow-on to the earlier Camel TF.1 ground attack aircraft (the TF designation standing for Trench Fighter) and replace the TF.1 in front line squadrons. It was powered by the same 230 hp Bentley nine cylinder rotary engine (with the 200 hp Clerget specified as an alternative engine) as the Snipe and had the same general appearance as the earlier fighter.

The aircraft was armed with a pair of .303 Vickers forward firing machine guns with 1,000 rounds per gun. The guns were mounted in a staggered arrangement with the starboard gun being some three inches ahead of the port weapon. This was done to allow the ammunition boxes to be installed side by side across the full width of the fuselage.

This was the second armament configuration, an earlier idea of mounting a pair of .303 Lewis guns pointing downward at about 45 degrees having been abandoned. Additionally, the Salamander carried four twenty-five pound Cooper bombs on under fuselage racks. Over the course of its development, the Salamander was used to test a number of armament options, including one Salamander that was experimentally fitted with an armament of eight downward firing Lewis machine guns.

RAF experience with the dangerous mission of ground attack, where service fighters had suffered almost thirty percent losses, led to the addition of some 605 pounds of armor plate on all sides of the cockpit, fuel tank and the installation of an armored headrest behind the cockpit. The front plate was 8MM thick, the side plates were 6 MM and the bottom plate was 11 MM thick. The rear wall was made of a six gauge plate over a ten gauge plate forming a double plate wall.

The Salamander differed from the Snipe in having a slab sided fuselage, fixed horizontal tail surfaces and the tapered armored headrest behind the cockpit. Late production Salamanders had the same horn balanced ailerons and enlarged fin and rudder found on the late production Snipe.

The first prototype Salamander was sent overseas during early May of 1918 for an operational evaluation. This evaluation was highly successful and the Salamander was ordered into production on a very large scale. By the end of October the RAF had thirty-seven on charge, although only two of these were in use over the Western Front. The RAF planned to equip four squadrons with the Salamander, Nos 86, 96, 157 and 158 and Nos 96 and 157 had begun to re-equip with the type when the war ended. Production continued after the war, well into the Summer of 1919 by which time more than 200 aircraft had been produced (many aircraft were reportedly put into long term storage after the war).

With its firepower, top speed of 125 mph and maneuverability, the potential shown by the Salamander was such that it was proposed that the aircraft be adopted as the standard post-war RAF fighter. In the event, another Sopwith product, the Snipe, was chosen for this role and no RAF squadron was equipped with Salamanders as its sole equipment.

One of the reasons the Salamander was rejected was a problem with warped armor plating. A lack of proper inspection and supervision of the armor plate being made for use on the Salamander led to a number of aircraft being built with warped armor. This, in turn, led to a misalignment of the fuselage, wings and tail plane. The misalignment led to serious control problems, rendering a number of aircraft unsafe for flight. This problem affected all the aircraft built and was not resolved until late 1919, although by that time it was no longer important.

The type was quickly withdrawn after the war, although a number of camouflaged Salamanders were sent to Egypt during 1922, no doubt as a result of the Chanak crisis. This crisis was sufficiently serious for at least one British newspaper to carry the headline "War Almost Inevitable."

One Salamander, F6533, was tested by the U.S. Air Services at McCook Field. The aircraft was carried on U.S. Army rolls until October of 1926.

**This Sopwith Salamander (E5429) trench fighter was sent to France during May of 1918 for an operational evaluation. Pilots reported that the Salamander was heavy on the controls.**

F6602, was one of 160 TF.2 Salamanders constructed at the Sopwith factory at Ham. The primary external difference between the Salamander and Snipe was the slab-sided fuselage of the Salamander.

This early production TF.2 Salamander still has the small vertical tail unit (fin and rudder) of the prototypes/early production aircraft.

It is believed that this is either an early production Salamander or one of the prototypes, as indicated by the small fin and rudder fitted to early aircraft. The fin and rudder were enlarged on production aircraft.

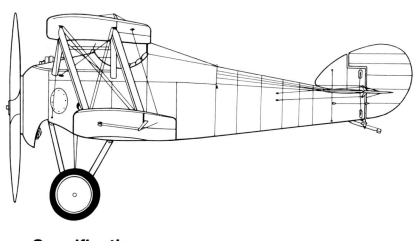

## Specifications

## Sopwith Salamander

Wingspan .................... 31 feet 2½ inches (w/balanced
                              ailerons)
Length ...................... 19 feet 6 inches
Height ...................... 9 feet 4 inches
Empty Weight ............... 1,844 pounds
Maximum Weight ............ 2,512 pounds
Powerplants ................. One 230 hp Bentley BR2 rotary
                              engine.

Armament .................... Two Vickers .303 machine guns with
                              1,000 rounds per gun.

Performance
  Maximum Speed ........... 125 mph
  Service ceiling ............. 13,000 feet
  Endurance ................ 2 hours
Crew ....................... One

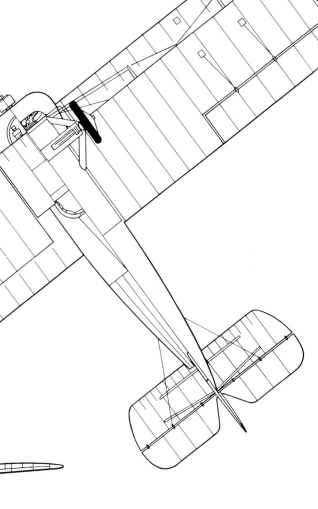

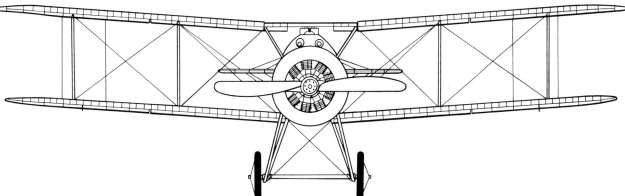

This Salamander (E5429) was inspected by Royal Navy personnel on 1 May 1918. The Royal Naval Air Service intended to use the Salamander for attack missions against naval targets.

The Salamander was a twin bay biplane with a very clean cowling for the 130 hp Bentley air-cooled radial engine. This aircraft is chocked on the airfield at Brooklands during the Salamander's test program.

The first prototype Salamander (E5429) was sent to France during May of 1918, stopping at Brooklands, Surrey while enroute. The aircraft had been modified with the staggered gun arrangement before departing for France.

One of the Salamander prototypes was used in camouflage experiments. Several schemes were tried including this one that featured different sizes for the upper wing roundels.

Sopwith Salamander TF.2 (E5429) departs for France on 9 May 1918 for its operational evaluation by No 1 Aeroplane Supply Depot. For the flight to the Continent the aircraft was flown by CAPT H. B. R. Rowell. The tests were conducted by CAPT G.Y. Tyrrel.

## Staggered Vickers Gun

### TF.2 Salamander

**Twin .303 Vickers**

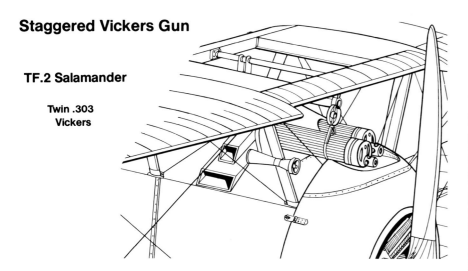

# Great equipment and units of the 20th century — the "in action" series from squadron signal.

## Land,

2027

3006

## Sea,

4003

## and Air.

1105